How to Face

Without Fear

Selections from the book
Preparation for Death
by St. Alphonsus Liguori

Adapted for modern readers
by
Norman J. Muckerman, C.SS.R.

LIGUORI
PUBLICATIONS

One Liguori Drive
Liguori, Missouri 63057
(314) 464-2500

Imprimi Potest:
Edmund T. Langton, C.SS.R.
Provincial, St. Louis Province
Redemptorist Fathers

Imprimatur:
+ George J. Gottwald
Vicar General, Archdiocese of St. Louis

ISBN 0-89243-029-X

Cover Photo: Norman J. Muckerman, C.SS.R.

In memory

of my mother,

who had to learn,

and my father,

who

somehow always knew.

Table of Contents

Foreword

We live today in a society which is not merely concerned with the fact of death; it has become heavily preoccupied with it.

In the past few years there have been more books written about this subject than for a full century before. Our magazines and journals report fully and faithfully the long discussions of learned people on death, as well as the drawn-out courtroom debates on a person's right to die. Schools and colleges report classrooms bulging with students taking courses on death.

In the words of the Madison Avenue marketers, death has suddenly become a "hot item."

More than 200 years ago, in 1758, St. Alphonsus Liguori published a book on death. He wrote it at age 62, after some 30 years of preaching about the subject on missions and retreats and of helping thousands of people prepare to meet their Maker. He called this book simply *Preparation for Death.*

In the foreword, Alphonsus said he wrote the book for a number of reasons. One was to offer solid, bedrock truths for readers who wished to meditate on death and thus lead better, holier lives. Another was to provide suitable material for preachers who, in his words, "have few books and little time for reading." For this reason, he liberally interlaced his own thoughts with quotations from the Scriptures and passages from early ecclesiastical writers — passages which are, as he said, "short, but strong and animated as they ought to be in sermons."

But mostly he wrote this book on death, as he did all his books, to bring people to the love of God, the gift and grace which brings with it all other graces, especially that of final perseverance. Alphonsus calls these two graces, namely divine love and final perseverance, the most important of all.

Not all of Alphonsus' *Preparation for Death* will be found in this volume. Some of the chapters, written for other generations and other peoples, have been omitted. Perhaps they would be overly dramatic for modern Christians. What has been selected, however, contains fundamental truths about death, truths which are based on God's own promises, on the words of Jesus, on the insights of many saints, especially of Alphonsus himself — all of which will, I hope, give us courage and be of immeasurable help in teaching us *How to Face Death Without Fear*.

Norman J. Muckerman, C.SS.R.

Feast of Mary, Mother of God
January 1, 1976

Chapter 1

Facing Death

" . . . It is appointed that men die once, and after death be judged" (Heb 9:27).

St. Augustine said it long ago: "Everything in our life, good or bad, is uncertain, except death; only death is certain." Of course, he was only pointing out a simple truth known to man from the beginning of time. As the Psalmist says, "What man shall live, and not see death?" (Ps 89:49)

We are born, says St. Cyprian, with a leash around our neck, and with every step we make we are led closer to death. To know that we must die, that after death there will be only heaven or hell, that on our death will depend eternal happiness or misery, and still refuse to take every possible means of securing a happy death, is surely the extreme of foolishness.

We must look into the face of death. How right are the decisions, how correct the actions of the person who judges and acts with the fact of his death in mind. A holy person was asked on his deathbed how he could be so cheerful. He replied: "I have always kept death before my eyes; now that it has arrived, I see nothing new in it."

A traveler would indeed be foolish if he thought only of acquiring wealth and honors in the countries he was passing through, knowing full well that he could not take them with him into his native land. And is he not a fool who seeks after happiness in a world which he is only passing through, where he will be only a short time, and all the while exposing himself to the risk of being unhappy for all eternity?

We do not become attached to things we borrow, because we know they must be returned to the owner. All the good things of this earth are in reality loaned to us. Why lose our heart to things we will soon have to give up anyway? Death strips us of all.

Prayer

O my God, up to now I have not thought too much about death, I have not looked into its face. And perhaps this is why I have offended you too much and have not loved you enough. But now I firmly resolve to serve you in earnest. Give me, O Lord, the strength to do so. Do not abandon me. You did not abandon me when I offended you; I therefore hope more confidently for your help now that I propose to serve you more faithfully.

Mary my Mother, you are the Mother of perseverance; obtain for me the grace to be faithful to my promise.

Chapter 2

Facing Death Without Fear

"But the souls of the just are in the hand of God, and no torment shall touch them . . . they are in peace" (Wis 3:1-3).

Nothing to Fear

The just have nothing to fear at the hour of death. If God holds them in his hands, who can snatch them from him? It is true that the powers of darkness try to tempt and attack even the saints at the hour of death. But it is also true that God continues to offer help — and even increases his graces — to his faithful servants at such a dangerous hour. As the Psalmist says: "The Lord is a stronghold . . . in times of distress" (Ps 9:10).

The servant of Elisha was struck with fear when he saw his city, Dothan, surrounded by the enemy. "What shall we do?" he said to the prophet. Elisha answered, "Do not be afraid . . . Our side outnumbers theirs" (2 Kgs 6:16).

So it is with the Christian facing death. The devil will come to tempt him, but his guardian angel will come to strengthen him. His patron saints and protectors will come as well as St. Michael, whom God has appointed as the defender of his faithful servants in their hour of death. Mary will come to protect her child who so often prayed to her for help "at the hour of death." And, above all, Jesus Christ himself will come to protect against all temptations those innocent or repentant sheep for whose salvation he died on the Cross. He will give the courage and strength needed in that last struggle.

Full of courage, then, the Christian will say: "The Lord is my light and my salvation; whom should I fear? The Lord is my life's refuge; of whom should I be afraid?" (Ps 27:1)

Origen says that God is more concerned about our salvation than the devil is for our destruction, because God loves us far more than the devil hates us.

" . . . God keeps his promise," says St. Paul. "He will not let you be tested beyond your strength . . ." (1 Cor 10:13). But you might ask: "Weren't there many saints who died with a great fear of being lost?" I answer that we have very few examples of this. And, even so, one author says, God sometimes permits holy people to be disturbed by such fears to purify them of some defect. As a general rule, God's faithful servants die in peace and joy. True, at death the thought of God's judgment causes fear in everyone. But while the unrepentant sinner passes from terror to a state of despair, the just rise from fear to confidence.

St. Bernard had such fears at the hour of his death. But he turned his thoughts to the merits of Jesus and overcame them. "Your wounds," he said to our Savior, "are my merits."

St. Hilarion also was fearful, but then he said to himself, "What are you afraid of? For seventy years you have served Christ; are you now afraid to die?"

Another holy man, a Jesuit priest, was asked on his deathbed if he still felt confident about death: "Have I spent my life serving Mohammed, that now I should doubt God's goodness or his desire to save me?"

If the thought of our past sins comes to trouble us at death, let us remember that God has stated that he forgets the offenses of repentant sinners. " . . . If the wicked man turns away from all the sins he committed . . . none of the crimes he committed shall be remembered against him . . ." (Ez 18:21-22).

You may ask, "How can I be sure of God's pardon?" St. Basil answers: He who says "I have hated and detested my sins" can be certain of pardon.

Jesus said: "He who obeys the commandments he has from me is the man who loves me . . . " (Jn 14:21). He who dies, then, obeying the commandments, dies in the love of God. And he who loves need not fear. "Love has no room for fear; rather, perfect love casts out all fear . . ." (1 Jn 4:18).

Peace, Sweet Peace

"They seemed, in the view of the foolish, to be dead . . . But they are in peace" (Wis 3:2). In the eyes of the unwise, God's faithful servants often seem to die, as irreligious people do, in sorrow and with reluctance. But the Father knows how to console his children in their last moments. Even in the midst of this suffering and pain, he pours into their souls a certain sweetness and peace as a foretaste of paradise.

Just as on their deathbed those who die in sin begin to experience certain foretastes of hell — remorse, fear, despair — so those who face death with God's love in their hearts begin to feel that peace which they will enjoy forever in heaven.

Father Suarez died in such peace that just before his death he exclaimed: "I could never imagine that death would be so sweet." When the doctor told Cardinal Baronius that he should not think so much about death, this holy man said: "Perhaps you think I am afraid of death. I fear it not; on the contrary, I love it." St. John Fisher, on seeing the scaffold where he was to be executed for the faith, said: "Walk swiftly, feet, we are not far from paradise!"

St. Francis of Assisi began to sing at the hour of his death and invited his brothers to join in. Brother Elias said to him, "Father, at death we ought to weep rather than sing." Replied Francis, "I can't stop singing, for I see I shall soon go to enjoy my God."

St. Teresa of Avila had such a strong desire to die and be with God that she looked upon life itself as death. And St. Ignatius of Antioch, who was sentenced to die by being devoured by wild animals, said that if the beasts should not want to kill him he would provoke them to do so, so great was his desire for heaven.

Foretaste of Heaven

"How can anyone fear death," says St. Cyprian, "when he is certain of paradise after death?" How can anyone fear death when he knows that by dying in the state of grace he will become immortal? "This mortal body [must be clothed] with immortality" (See 1 Cor 15:53).

He who faces death in the grace of God can hope soon to see Jesus Christ and to hear from him these consoling words: " . . . Well done! You are an industrious and reliable servant. Since you were dependable in a small matter I will put you in charge of large affairs. Come, share your master's joy!" (Mt 25:21)

Oh, what comfort he will then receive from all his good works, his prayers, his penances, from all he has done for God." "Happy the just, for it will be well with them, the fruit of their works they will eat" (Is 3:10).

What special consolations will be offered the just servant of God at the hour of death for all the devotions performed in honor of Mary, the Mother of God. Mary is called "Virgin most faithful" — how faithfully will she console her servant at the hour of death!

How great will be the joy of those who have in life loved Jesus, who have often visited him in the Most Blessed Sacrament, received him so frequently in Holy Communion, when they see this same Lord as Viaticum, coming to accompany them in the passage to eternity! Like St. Philip Neri, they will say: "Behold my love! Behold my love! Give me my love."

But you might say, "Who knows what will be my lot? Maybe I will die an unhappy death!" Let me ask you:

What causes a bad death? Only sin! We should then fear only sin and not death. If you desire not to fear death, lead a holy life. "He who fears the Lord will have a happy end . . . " (Sir 1:11).

Father Colombiére held it to be morally impossible for a person who was faithful to God during life to die a bad death. And, before him, St. Augustine said: "He who has lived well cannot die badly. He who is prepared to die fears no death, however sudden."

Those who offer their death to God make the most perfect act of divine love possible, because by cheerfully accepting the kind of death which God is pleased to send when and how God sends it, they are just like the holy martyrs who died for Christ's sake.

Let us use our life only to advance in divine love. The level of our love for God at death will be the level of our love for him in a happy eternity.

Prayer

My Jesus, bind me to yourself so that I may never more be separated from you. Make me entirely yours before I die. I wish to love you ardently in this life, that I may love you ardently in the next. If in the past I have not loved you as I should, now I turn to you with all my heart and soul. Give me, sweet Jesus, holy perseverance and grant me, also, the grace always to ask for it. Mary, my Mother, assist me now and at the hour of my death.

Chapter 3

No Lasting City

"Man goes to his lasting home . . . " (Eccl 12:5).

Many centuries ago, men with no clear idea of the supernatural, but using only the light of reason, observed that on this earth so many wicked people live in prosperity and comfort, while so many good persons suffer. Therefore, they said since there is a just God, there must be another life where the wicked are punished and the good rewarded.

What they learned by the light of reason, we Christians know by the light of faith. St. Paul tells us: " For here we have no lasting city; we are seeking one which is to come" (Heb 13:14).

This earth is certainly not our true and final home. It is at best a kind of hotel, a hospital, a wayfarer's inn, from which we shall be discharged or forced to depart, perhaps at the time when we least expect. It would be the height of foolishness for someone who knows he is only a pilgrim to spend all his fortune to purchase a large estate in a country through which he is merely passing, and which he must leave in a few days.

What then is man's final destiny? Scripture says: "Man goes to his lasting home."

The prophet says: "Man goes" to show that each one of us shall go into the home he himself shall choose. He shall not be carried to it, but will go of his own will. It is certain that God wills the salvation of all men, but he will not save us by force. He has placed before each of us life or death. The choice is ours.

Here on earth we must always remember that eternity is at stake. When a man builds a house for himself and his family, he will go to extremes to find the best location. He will plan carefully, he will seek to make his home comfortable and beautiful. Why then are people so careless about the home where they must dwell for all eternity?

When Thomas More, who had been friend of Henry VIII and Lord Chancellor of England, was awaiting death in the Tower of London, his wife visited him. She begged him to yield to the wishes of the King, and thus save his life. "Tell me," he said to her gently, "how many more years do you think I shall still live?" "Another twenty or so for sure," she replied. "My dear," said the saint, "for twenty more years of life here on earth do you want me to forfeit my chances for an eternity of happiness?"

We need this kind of vision, this kind of faith. If eternity were only a doubtful matter, something based only on a probability, we should still make every effort to lead a good life, lest this teaching be true and we should lose all. But there are no doubts about eternity; it is infallibly certain; it is a truth of faith.

We say: We believe *in life everlasting*. Let us then use every means of strengthening this faith and of arriving at this eternal life. To obtain it, no effort should be too great.

Prayer

Oh my God, I know that there is no middle way. I will either be forever happy in heaven, or forever miserable in hell. I know that through sin I have already deserved hell. But I also know that you pardon all who repent and you save from hell those who hope in you. Of

this you assure me: "He shall call upon me; and . . . I will deliver him and glorify him" (Ps 91:15).

Oh sovereign God, I am most sorry for having offended you. Restore me to your grace and give me your holy love. Never permit me to be separated from you again.

Mary my Mother, assist me by your prayers!

Chapter 4

The Shortness of Life

". . . You are a vapor that appears briefly and vanishes" (Jas 4:14).

All of us know that we must die. But the delusion of many is that they imagine death as far-off, as if it will never come. But Job tells us that life is short. "Man born of woman is short-lived and full of trouble. Like a flower that springs up and fades . . . " (Jb 14:1). Again Job says: "My days are swifter than a runner, they flee away . . . " (Jb 9:25).

Death runs to meet us, and we at every moment run toward death. Every step, every breath bring us nearer to the end of life.

How do those who do not think about the shortness of life and are consequently unprepared for death act in the face of death? Usually they wish to speak only of their illness and pain, or of getting other physicians to attend them, or new and better drugs to cure them. If you try to talk to them about the state of their soul, they will soon grow weary or complain of a headache or say that it pains them to hear anyone speak.

Truly, life is short, and death, like a lighted candle, makes the "good things" of life appear as they really are. Of what use are any of them when all that remains for a person is the darkness of the grave?

Let us persuade ourselves that the right time for doing something about our spiritual recklessness is not at the hour of death, but while we are still healthy and strong. Let us do now what we will be unable to do then.

Antisthenes, a pagan, when asked what was the greatest blessing a man could receive in this life, answered: "A good death." What will the Christian, enlightened by faith, say? If you believe that you must die, that there is an eternity, that you die only once, and that if you make a mistake then, your mistake is unpardonable, why do you not at this very moment begin to do everything possible to make sure you die a good death? Begin now to live a life which will be at the hour of death a source not of fear and affliction, but of peace and consolation.

Prayer

Oh Jesus, my Savior, you redeemed me by dying for me. Yet even then you foresaw my sins and my ingratitude. Still, in my blindness you have given me light. I lost you, and you enabled me to find you. Merciful Savior, make me feel the great debt I owe you and give me a great sorrow for my sins.

Chapter 5

The Fact of Death

" . . . You are dirt, and to dirt you shall return" (Gn 3:19).

Consider that you are dust and that you shall return to dust. The day will come when you shall have to die. The same lot awaits everyone, the rich and the poor, the strong and the weak, the good and the bad. At the moment of death, the moment when your soul leaves your body, it shall go to eternity, and the body shall return to dust.

See what death does to a person. Before death, he might have been admired, even sought after; now he is something that must be gotten rid of and quickly buried in the earth. During life, he might have been well known and esteemed for his clever wit, his polish, his pleasing presence, his intelligence and wisdom; but after death he is soon forgotten.

When people hear of his death, some might remark: "He was a good man." Others may say, "He provided well for his children." Some might regret his death because during life he was of great use to them; others will rejoice at his death because it will be to their own advantage. But in a little while no one will speak of him any more. For a few days after his death, his nearest relatives will shrink from hearing his name, through fear of renewing their grief. But they will soon be consoled by the thoughts of their share of his estate.

Thus, in a short time his death will even be a source of joy. In the very home in which he died, in the very room where he was judged by Jesus Christ, others will dance and eat and play and laugh as before. And where will his soul be then?

In this picture of death see yourself and what must happen to you one day. Remember: "You are dirt, and to dirt you shall return."

All must end; and if at death you lose your soul, all will be lost for you.

When St. Camillus saw a cemetery and looked at the graves of the dead, he said to himself: "If these could return to life, what would they not do to get to heaven?

What do we do, we who still have time? Remember the fig tree of which Jesus said: "Look here! For three years now I have come in search of fruit on this fig tree, and found none" (Lk 13:7).

We have been in the world for more than three years. What fruits have we produced? Let us learn to profit in the time which God in his mercy still gives us. We cannot wait until we are told that there is no more time or that the time for leaving this world has arrived. We must be ready to die today, now, at this very moment!

Prayer

Oh my God, I am that tree which for so many years has deserved to hear from you the words: "Cut it down. Why does it clutter up the ground?" Yes, up till now, I have brought forth no fruit other than the thorns of sin. Still, Lord, you do not wish that I despair. You have said to all that whoever seeks you shall find you. "Seek, and you will find." You have also said: "Anything you ask me in my name, I will do." My Jesus, trusting in this great promise, I ask in your name and through your merits for your grace and your love. Grant that grace and love may abound in my soul where sin has heretofore abounded.

Chapter 6

The Death of the Good Person

"Precious in the eyes of the Lord is the death of his faithful ones" (Ps 116:15).

Death Brings Peace

When viewed only in the light of the senses, death can excite fear and terror. But if we look at it with the eyes of faith, death is consoling and even desirable.

St. Bernard says, "Death is the end of labors, the consumation of victory, the gate of life. Death brings an end to toil and labor." "Man," says Job, "born of a woman, is short-lived and full of trouble." To the good person, death brings peace and happiness. " . . . Happy now are the dead who die in the Lord . . . " (Rv 14:13).

In the Book of Wisdom we read, "The souls of the just are in the hand of God, and no torment shall touch them." The command to leave this world, which is so full of terror for those who love the world, does not alarm good people. They are not afflicted at the thought of having to leave riches, possessions, wealth, the goods of the earth, for they have never been attached to them. They do not fear giving up worldly honors and dignities, for they have always hated them or considered them to be what in truth they are — vanity and smoke! Neither are they afflicted in leaving their relatives and friends, for they loved them only in God. Now in death they recommend them to the heavenly Father who loves them more than they do. So, trusting that their own salvation is secure, they expect to be better able to help them from heaven than they did on earth.

Thus good people can die in peace and happiness, saying with the Psalmist: "As soon as I lie down, I fall peacefully asleep, for you alone, O Lord, bring security to my dwelling" (Ps 4:9).

Death Is Victory

The greatest consolation which a person who has loved God will experience on hearing the news of death will come from the thought that soon he will be delivered from the many dangers of offending God. Likewise, death will bring an end to temptation, troubles of conscience, the unceasing warfare with hell, in which we are in continual danger of losing our soul and God. The thought of being freed by death from the danger of sin consoled St. Teresa and made her rejoice, as often as she heard the clock strike, that another hour of trial had passed.

St. Paul esteemed death his greatest gain, because by death he acquired that life which never ends. "For to me, 'life' means Christ; hence dying is so much gain" (Phil 1:21). The person who lives in union with God in this life is happy and blessed. But, as a sailor is not safe and secure until he has arrived in port and escaped the storm, so a person cannot enjoy complete happiness until he has left this world in the grace of God. If as he nears port the sailor rejoices, how much greater ought to be the joy and gladness of a Christian who is at the point of obtaining or securing eternal salvation?

Entrance to Life

St. Bernard says that death is not only the end of labors; it is also the gate of life. He who wishes to see God must necessarily pass through this gate.

When St. Charles Borromeo saw in his house a painting which showed death with a scythe in its hand, he sent for a painter and ordered him to erase the scythe and paint instead a golden key. Thus he wished to be more and more inflamed with a desire of death which opens paradise and admits us to the vision of God.

When Simeon held the infant Jesus in his arms, he asked no other grace than to be delivered from this present life. "Now, Master, you can dismiss your servant in peace." St. Paul desired the same grace when he said: "I long to be freed from this life and to be with Christ, for that is the far better thing" (Phil 1:23).

For this reason the day of the death of a saint is called his birthday, because at death a saint is born to a life of happiness which will never end.

This is, as was promised by the prophet, Hosea, the grace which Jesus Christ merited for us. By dying for us, Jesus has changed death into life.

Prayer

Oh my God, I have dishonored you by turning my back upon you. But your Son has honored you by offering you the sacrifice of his life on the Cross. Through the honor which your beloved Son has given you, pardon the dishonor which I have done to you. If I have dishonored you in the past, I hope to honor you for eternity by blessing and praising your mercy forever. Oh my God, I ask only to love you and hope always to ask to love you until, dying in your love, I reach the kingdom of love where, without needing to ask it any more, I shall be full of love for all eternity. Mary, my Mother, obtain for me the grace to love God ardently in this life, that I may love him ardently forever in the next.

Chapter 7

How to Prepare for Death

"In whatever you do, remember your last days, and you will never sin" (Sir 7:36).

Do Not Wait Until the Last Minute

We all know that we must die, and die only once, and that nothing is more important for us than to die a good death. On our death depends whether we shall be forever happy in heaven or forever lost in hell. We know too that our eternal happiness or unhappiness will depend on whether we lead a good or bad life. How does it happen then that so many Christians live as though they were never going to die? Or as if to die a good or a bad death is of little importance? They live in sin because they do not think of death. "Remember your last days, and you will never sin."

We must be convinced that the hour of death is not a good time for settling our spiritual accounts and for gaining eternal salvation. Businessmen will always take prudent measures in ample time to acquire financial gains. Sick people do not put off taking the medicines needed to preserve or to restore their health. A person on trial for his life will not delay preparation for his trial until the day of the trial itself. Military leaders would be considered foolish if they would put in a supply of provisions and arms only when their position was under seige. Far more foolish is the Christian who would neglect settling his conscience until the moment of death.

In the Book of Proverbs we read: "When terror comes upon you like a storm, and your doom approaches like a whirlwind; when distress and anguish befall you. Then they call me, but I answer not; they seek me, but find me not" (Prv 1:27-28). The time of death is a time of storm and whirlwind. At that awful hour sinners will call on God for assistance, but they invoke his aid through fear of hell, which they see threatening, and not with true contrition of heart. It is for this reason that God will not answer. What they have sown they shall reap.

It will not then be enough merely to receive the sacraments. It is necessary at death to hate sin and to love God above all things. But how can he who has loved forbidden pleasures all his life hate them at the moment of death? How can he who all during life has loved creatures more than he has loved God begin to love him above all things at that moment?

What anguish will the sinner feel when he hears the words: " . . . What is this I hear about you? Give me an account of your service, for it is about to come to an end" (Lk 16:2). Then there will be no more time for doing penance, for receiving the sacraments, for visiting Christ in the Holy Eucharist, or for prayer. What is done is done. To make a good confession and thus ease his conscience would require a better state of mind and time free from confusion and agitation. But time will be no more.

Examine Your Conscience and Straighten out Your Life

Since it is certain that you will die, you should go as quickly as possible to Jesus and thank him for the time which in his mercy he gives you to settle your conscience. Then review your past life. Recall God's commandments. Examine yourself on how you have lived according to them. Examine yourself also on the duties of your vocation in life. Recall as fully as possible the sins you may have committed and go to confession with full sorrow. Remember that you must settle your accounts for eternity; try to adjust them now as if you were on the point of giving "an account of your service" to Jesus Christ at judgment.

Banish from your heart all sinful affections and every feeling of anger and hatred for others. Resolve to avoid all those occasions of sin in which you would be in danger of losing God. Remember that what now appears difficult will seem impossible at the hour of death.

Even more important is the resolution to adopt the means of keeping yourself in God's grace. These means are many. They would include, for example, hearing Mass frequently, meditating on the eternal truths, receiving the sacraments of the Eucharist and Penance frequently, visiting the Most Blessed Sacrament and our Lady, reading the Sacred Scriptures and other spiritual books, examining your conscience daily, and having some special devotion to the Blessed Mother. Above all determine to recommend yourself to God and to the Blessed Mother, especially in time of temptation, by calling upon the sacred names of Jesus and Mary. These are the names by which you will be able to gain a happy death and everlasting life.

If you adopt this way of life and place great confidence in Jesus and Mary, you will receive great helps from God and acquire strength of soul. If you give yourself to God, who invites you, you will begin to enjoy that peace of mind of which you have been deprived up till now through your own fault. What greater peace can a person enjoy than to be able to say, upon retiring, that if death should come this night, he will die in the grace of God.

Detach Yourself from Worldly Affections

We must try to be at all times in the state in which we desire to be at death. "Happy now are the dead who die in the Lord!" (Rv 14:13) St. Ambrose says that those who are dead to worldly affections during life will die a good death. We must accept in life the loss of goods, friends, relatives, in fact all the things of this world. Unless we do this on our own during life, we shall be forced to do it at death, and then it will be with great pain and even greater danger of eternal perdition.

St. Augustine says that settling earthly affairs during life and disposing of all earthly goods, at least by making a will, will contribute greatly to a peaceful death. When all of our earthly concerns are in order, we can be entirely occupied in uniting ourselves with God. At the hour of death, we should be thinking and speaking only of God and of heaven. These last moments are too precious to be squandered in earthly thoughts.

Examine yourself today to see if you are too attached to anything on this earth, to any person, to any honor, to your home, to your money, to amusements. Then remember that you are mortal. One day, and perhaps very soon, you will be forced to leave all these things. Why then should you have any undue attachment to them, and thus expose yourself to the danger of an unhappy death? From this moment offer everything to God and tell him that you are ready to give up all things whenever he wishes to take them from you or you from them.

Spend every day as if it were the last of your life; perform every action, every prayer, make every Holy Communion, as if they were the last of your life. Imagine yourself at the point of death. How powerfully will this thought help you to walk in the way of God and to detach your heart from earthly affections. "Happy that servant whom his master discovers at work on his return!" (Mt 24:26) He who expects death every hour will die well, even though death should come suddenly upon him.

Prayer

My God, I wish to love you to the utmost of my power here on earth, that I may love you more perfectly in heaven. I offer you all that I have, but especially the

pains and the sacrifice of my life in union with the sacrifice which Jesus offered for me on the Cross. The pains which I suffer are few and light compared to what I really deserve. But I embrace them, such as they are, as a mark of the love which I bear you. I know that because I have so often despised your love, I deserved never more to love you; but you cannot reject a penitent soul. I am sorry, O Sovereign Good, for having offended you. Now I love you with my whole heart and place all my trust in you. Your death, O my Redeemer, is my hope. Into your wounded hands I assign myself. "Into your hands I commend my spirit . . . " (Ps 31:6).

Chapter 8
Discovering True Values

"What profit would a man show if he were to gain the whole world and destroy himself in the process?" (Mt 16:26)

An ancient philosopher named Aristippus once suffered shipwreck and lost all his belongings. He was rescued, however, and his rescuers, because of his fame and learning, tried to replace all he had lost. Later he wrote to his friends and told them to put themselves in his situation and to seek only those things which would not be taken away from them by shipwreck.

Our relatives and friends who have already died would offer us, from eternity, the same advice. Death is called the day of "requital" in Scripture (Dt 32:35), because, on the day we die, we shall lose earthly goods — honor, riches, pleasures. St. Ambrose says that we cannot take them with us into eternity. Our virtues alone will accompany us into the next life.

Jesus asks what will it profit us to gain the whole world if at death we lose all this and heaven too. How many people have made this thought the guideline of their lives and the reason for giving themselves entirely to God? It was by this truth that St. Ignatius drew many souls to God, particularly Francis Xavier who was, at the time, living a worldly life in Paris. "Francis," Ignatius said one day, "the world is a traitor; it promises but does not perform. But even if it did make you happy, how long would this last? Longer than your life? And after death, what will you take into eternity? Where is the rich man who has ever brought with him the smallest coin or a servant to attend him in eternity?" Francis Xavier left Paris, followed Ignatius, and became a saint.

The author of the Book of Ecclesiastes says: "Nothing that my eyes desired did I deny them, nor did I deprive myself of any joy, but my heart rejoiced in the fruit of all my toil. This was my share for all my toil. But when I turned to all the works that my hands had wrought and to the toil at which I had taken such pains, behold, all was vanity and a chase after wind, with nothing gained under the sun" (Eccl 2:10-11).

How really valuable, then, are earthly goods? Or how worthy are they of our faith and trust?

The prophet Hosea spoke of the "merchant who holds a false balance, who loves to defraud!" (Hos 12:8) The world is such a merchant, and worldly goods are fraudulent; they cannot truly satisfy our hearts. They end too soon. Job said, "My days are swifter than a runner, they flee away . . . They shoot by like skiffs of reed, like an eagle swooping upon its prey" (Jb 9:25-26).

The days of our lives pass, fly away, and of all our worldly goods and pleasures, what will we keep? Ask so many of the rich and learned, the princes, presidents, and kings who are now in eternity, what they possess now of all the riches, the pomp, the delights, the power they enjoyed here on earth. They will all answer, Nothing, nothing. "What did our pride avail us?" they will say with the author of the Book of Wisdom. "What have wealth and its boastfulness afforded us? All of them passed like a shadow and like a fleeting rumor; like a ship traversing the heaving water of which, when it has passed, no trace can be found, no path of its keel in the waves" (Wis 5:10).

True values become more clear in the light of the death candle. At the hour of his death, Pope Leo XI said: "Oh, that I had left the world and led a life of sanctity. It would have been better for me to have been doorkeeper in my monastery than the Pope of Rome." When Philip II, King of Spain, was dying, he called for his son and, pulling aside his royal robes, showed the young prince the horrible sores covering his body. "See," he said, "how even kings die and how the grandeurs of this world end. Now I wish I had been a religious and not a king!"

St. Teresa of Avila says that a true and honest life means living in such a way as not to have any reason to fear death. If, then, we wish to see the true value of things, let us look at them as if from our deathbed. We will then seek to become rich in those goods which will accompany us to the other world and make us happy for all eternity.

But, let us also do this right away. St. Paul tells us: ". . . The time is short . . . The world as we know it is passing away" (1 Cor 7:29-31). We must try to live in such a way that what was said to the fool in the Gospel story will not be said to us on our deathbed, " . . . You fool! This very night your life shall be required of you." Then Jesus concluded, "That is the way it works with the man who grows rich for himself instead of growing rich in the sight of God" (Lk 12:20-21).

Jesus said, "Make it your practice instead to store up heavenly treasure, which neither moths nor rust corrode nor thieves break in and steal" (Mt 6:20).

Let us strive to acquire the great treasure of God's love. St. Augustine says, "What does the rich man have, if he has not the love of God? What does the poor man need, if he has this love?" If a man has all the riches in the world and has not God, he is the poorest of men. But the poor man who possesses God, possesses all things.

" . . . He who abides in love abides in God, and God in him" (1 Jn 4:16).

Prayer

O Jesus, my Redeemer, you have suffered so much pain, such great ignominy for my sake! And I have loved

the pleasures and the goods of this earth to such a degree that, to have them, I have often forgotten you and trampled upon your grace.

But since you continued to pursue me, even after I despised you, I cannot fear that you will reject me now that I seek you and wish to love you with all my heart and am sorry for having offended you.

I accept, now, all the pains and sufferings which may come into my life. Let me suffer with you in this life that in the next I may rejoice with you and love you for all eternity.

Mary, my Mother, to you I recommend my life. Pray to Jesus for me always.

Chapter 9
The Value of Time

"Use your time well; guard yourself from evil" (Sir 4:20).

Time — the Greatest Gift

In this life, the greatest gift God can give us is time. Even the pagans of old knew the value of time. Seneca called time a "priceless gift."

The saints have understood its value even more. St. Bernardine of Sienna, for example, says that a moment of time is as valuable as God himself, because in one moment a person can, by an act of sorrow or of love, win the grace of God and even heaven.

We hold this treasure only for our present life. It does not exist in the next, neither in hell nor in heaven. Those who are in hell now would pay any price just to have one hour of time to repair themselves; but this hour they will never have. There are no tears in heaven, but if those who are in heaven could weep, they would do so for having lost time on earth which they could have used to become even more holy, time which they no longer can have.

How do you spend your time? Why do you always put off until tomorrow what you could do today? Remember that time past is yours no longer; remember too that you have no claim to the future. You have only the present to do good. St. Bernard asks, "Why do you count on the future, as if God has placed time in your power?" And St. Augustine says, "You are not sure of even another hour of life; how can you promise yourself tomorrow?"

If then, concludes St. Teresa, you are not ready to die today, fear lest you die an unhappy death later!

Neglect of Time

Nothing is more precious than time, yet nothing is less esteemed, nothing more neglected. St. Bernard remarks: The days of salvation pass by and no one reflects that they will never come again.

Some people spend days and nights doing little or nothing. If you ask them what they are doing, their answer is that they are just killing time.

Others spend hours in long conversations on useless or even obscene subjects. If you ask them what they are doing the answer is the same: killing time.

Poor blind people who lose so much time — time which will never be theirs again!

Yet when death draws near, how these people will beg God for more time! Just another year, another month, even another day — but they will not get it. For them, there will be no more time!

Ecclesiastes says: "Remember your Creator in the days of your youth, before the evil days come . . . before the sun is darkened . . ." (Eccl 12:1-2).

How great is the distress and disappointment of the traveler who when night falls discovers that he has taken the wrong road, and he has no time left to correct his mistake. Such will be the anguish of those who come to die realizing that they have lived many years on earth, but not for God.

" . . . The night comes on when no one can work" (Jn 9:4). That night is death.

Using Time Well

Jesus answered: "The light is among you only a little longer. Walk while you still have it or darkness will come over you . . . " (Jn 12:35). We must walk in the way of the Lord during life, while we have light. The time of death is not the time to start preparing for eternity, but the time for being ready.

If a person were advised that in a short time he would have to stand trial, and in this trial, he could possibly lose all he owned on earth and even his life, he certainly would waste no time or effort to find the best lawyer to represent him. He surely would do everything he could to win a favorable judgment.

What about ourselves? We know for certain that a most important trial — involving our eternal destiny — will soon be held. The decision may be handed down at any hour. Yet we still waste time!

Someone might say: I am still young; I will give myself to God, to religion later on.

Such a one should remember that Jesus cursed the fig tree the *first* time he found it without fruit, even out of season. By this he wished to teach us that we must always — even in our youth — be fruitful in good works.

In Revelation we read: " . . . Woe to you, earth and sea, for the devil has come down upon you! His fury knows no limits, for he knows his time is short" (Rv 12:12). If the devil loses no time in trying to get us to hell, should we lose time in trying to assure our eternal salvation and in making sure we get to heaven?

Others will say: "I'm not doing anything wrong!" I ask, is it not wrong to "kill time?" Does God give us time that we may squander it?

In the Book of Sirach we read, "Work at your tasks in due season" (Sir 51:30). And Jesus, in the story of the laborers in the vineyard, has the master of the vineyard rebuking those men who stood around the marketplace idle! All time not spent in some way for God is lost time!

Consider too that at each moment of time we may gain new treasures of eternal wealth. If you were promised all the money you could count in one day, or all the land you could walk around in one day, would you not immediately count the money as fast as you could? Wouldn't you *run* to cover as much land as you could?

Do not say that you will do tomorrow what you could do today. For today will then be lost forever, and it will never return.

Prayer

My God, I will no longer lose the time which you in your mercy give me. I thank you for having preserved my life. And since I still have time to ask your graces, I ask for these two in particular: Give me perseverance in grace, and give me your love. After that, you can do with me whatever you will!

Chapter 10
God's Love for Us

"We love . . . because he first loved us" (1 Jn 4:19).

The Love and Goodness of God for Us

God deserves your love because he has loved you before you loved him. He has been the first of all to love you. "With age-old love I have loved you . . . " (Jer 31:3).

Your parents were the first to love you on this earth, but they loved you only after they knew you. Before your father and mother were even born, God loved you. Even before the world was created, he loved you. It is useless to count the years or ages that God has loved you, for as he himself says, "I have loved you with an age-old love" (see Jer 31:3).

As long as God has been God, he has loved you. As long as he has loved himself, he has loved you. This is why the holy virgin, St. Agnes, when the pagan emperor tried to make her reject God and marry a rich Roman nobleman, said, "I have another and previous lover."

God has, then, loved you from eternity and because of this love has taken you from so many others whom he could have created. He gave you existence. He placed you in this world. Out of love for you he also created many other beautiful things, that they might serve you and remind you of his love for you and the love you owe to him. St. Augustine used to say: "Heaven and earth tell me to love you." When he looked at the sun, the moon, the stars, the mountains, the rivers, they cried out to him: "Augustine, love your God, for he has created us for you, that you might love him."

Abbot de Rancé, founder of the Trappists, would say, when he saw a hill, a fountain, or a flower, that these creatures reproached him for his ingratitude to God. When St. Mary Magdalene de Pazzi held a flower or a fruit in her hand, she would say within herself, "My God has from eternity thought of creating this flower, this fruit, that I might love him."

Moreover, God has shown you special love in allowing you to be born as a Christian, in the true faith, in a society where you can freely worship him. How many people are born without this gift? The number of those who are so fortunate as to be born in a part of the world where the true faith exists is small, compared to the rest of mankind. And God has chosen you to be one of that small number.

What an infinite gift is the gift of faith! Think of all the people who are deprived of the sacraments, of the examples of good, Christian living, and of all the other helps to salvation that are found in the Christian faith.

And God has given all these helps to you without any merit or love on your part, and even with the foreknowledge of your own failure to love him fully. For when he thought of creating you and bestowing all these graces upon you, he foresaw that sometimes you would fail to love him as you should.

God Gives Himself

Not only has God given us so many beautiful creatures, much more he gave us himself. "He gave himself for us" (Eph 5:2). Sin robbed us of divine grace and made us liable to eternal death, but the Son of God came on earth to redeem us from eternal death and gain for us the grace and eternal happiness which we had lost.

" . . . He emptied himself and took the form of a slave, being born in the likeness of men" (Phil 2:7).

God born in the likeness of men! "The Word became flesh" (see Jn 1:14). But our amazement must increase when we contemplate all that Jesus has done and suffered for love of us. To redeem us, it would have been enough for him to shed one single drop of his blood or one single tear or offer only one prayer. But, says St. John Chrysostom, "What was sufficient for our redemption was not sufficient for the immense love which God bore for us. He not only wished to save us but, because he loved us so much, he wished to be loved ardently in return. Therefore, he resolved to lead a life full of sorrow and pain and to suffer the most painful of all deaths, in order to make us understand the infinite love which he has for us." St. Paul wrote: "And it was thus that he humbled himself, obediently accepting even death, death on a cross" (Phil 2:8).

All men and all angels will never be able to comprehend this excess of divine love. St. Bonaventure called the Passion of Christ an "excess of sorrow and of love." If Jesus had not been God, but a friend or a relative, what greater proof of love could he have given than to die for us? "There is no greater love than this: to lay down one's life for one's friends" (Jn 15:13).

If Jesus had to save his own Father, he could not have done more than he did for us. If you had been God and Father of Jesus Christ, what more could he have done for you than sacrifice his life amid so much torment and pain, for the love of you? If the most unlovable man on earth had done for you what Jesus Christ has done, could you live without loving him?

Before the Incarnation, man might have doubted whether God loved him so much. But after the Incarnation and death of Jesus Christ, how can anyone doubt any longer that God loves him with the most tender love? What greater affection could he show you than to sacrifice his divine life for the love of you?

The Passion and Death of Jesus Reveal God's Love

Our astonishment must increase when we consider the desire that Jesus had to suffer and die for love of us. "I have a baptism to receive. What anguish I feel till it is over!" (Lk 12:50) The baptism that Jesus was to receive was the baptism of his own blood. He desired that his Passion and Death should come soon, that man would soon know the great love he bore for him. It was this desire that made Jesus say, on the night before his Passion: ". . . I have greatly desired to eat this Passover with you before I suffer" (Lk 22:15).

How is it possible for us to live without loving God when we consider that he died for our sake, and with such a great desire of showing his love for us? "The love of Christ impels us . . . " (2 Cor 5:14). St. Paul says that it is not so much what Jesus has done and suffered for us and our salvation as it is the love which he showed in suffering for us that calls and even forces us to love him.

Who could ever believe, unless assured of it by faith, that the Creator would die for his own creatures? St. Mary Magdalene de Pazzi, holding a crucifix in her hands, exclaimed, "My Jesus, you are a fool, a fool because of love." This is what the gentiles said when they heard the apostles preaching on the death of Jesus Christ. As St. Paul tells us, they regarded it as foolishness, something that could not be believed. "We preach Christ crucified — a stumbling block to Jews, and an absurdity to gentiles" (1 Cor 1:23).

How could a God who is most happy himself, who stands in need of no one, come to earth to become man and die for the love of mankind who are his own creatures? This would be the same as to say that God surely became foolish for the sake of men. But our faith teaches us that Jesus Christ, the true Son of God, has delivered himself to death for love of us. "He loved us and gave himself for us" (see Eph 5:2).

Why has he done this? He did it so that we might no

longer live for ourselves but for him who died for us. "He died for all so that those who live might live no longer for themselves, but for him who for their sake died and was raised up" (2 Cor 5:15). He did it so that, through the love which he has shown us, he might win our love. "That is why Christ died and came to life again, that he might be Lord of both the dead and the living" (Rom 14:9).

This is why the saints, contemplating the death of Jesus, thought it very little to give up everything they had and even their lives for the love of so loving a God. How many Christians, rich, poor, princes, paupers, young, old, have given up their families, their riches, their lives, their pleasures, and have given themselves to Jesus in life and even in death, in order thus to make some small return for the love of this God who has died for their sake! And you, what have you done up till now in return for the love of Jesus Christ? As he has died for the saints — for a St. Lucy, a St. Laurence, a St. Agnes, so he has also died for you. What do you intend to do during the days that remain for you on earth, days which God gives you so that you may love him? From this day forward look often at the crucifix and, as you do, call to mind the love which Jesus Christ has shown you. Then say within yourself, "My Jesus, you have died for me. You have died for love of me. Help me to love a God who has loved me so tenderly."

Prayer

My Jesus, my Redeemer, I have not loved you because I have not thought enough of the love which you have shown me. I have been very ungrateful to you. You have given your life for me in the most painful of all deaths; have I been so ungrateful as not even to think of your sufferings? Pardon me now. I promise that from this day forward I will remember your love and the pains which you endured for my sake, that I may love you and nevermore offend you. I have lived long enough unmind-

ful of your sufferings and of your love. From now on may I think of nothing else, speak of nothing else, do nothing else, than love you.

Mary, my Mother, make me love your Son more and more.

Chapter 11
Our Merciful Father

". . . Mercy triumphs over judgment" (Jas 2:13).

God Waits

Goodness, by nature, gives of itself. It is naturally inclined to communicate itself to others. God, who by his nature is infinite goodness, has an infinite desire to share his happiness with us. This is why he wishes not to punish us but to show mercy toward us.

When God punishes us in this life, he does it in order to show mercy in the next. When he chastises us, it is because he loves us and wants to save us from eternal punishment.

Consider the great mercy of God in waiting for our repentance. He could have struck us dead when we offended him. Instead, he waited for us; he preserved our life; he even pretended not to see our sins.

Isaiah says that God waits for sinners. "The Lord is waiting to show you favor, and he rises to pity you. For the Lord is a God of justice" (Is 30:18).

Why all this patience on God's part? He tells us: "I take no pleasure in the death of the wicked man, but rather in the wicked man's conversion, that he may live" (Ez 33:11).

St. Augustine goes so far as to say that God, if he were not God, would be unjust because of his excessive patience toward sinners.

God Calls

When Adam rebelled against God and hid himself, God went in search for him and called out to him sorrowfully: "Adam, where are you?" These are the words of a father seeking a lost son.

God still does the same for us. We have fled from his face, yet he seeks us, calling us by his inspiration, by remorse of conscience, by something we might hear in a sermon, by sickness or trials, or even by the death of someone dear to us. He could say in the words of the Psalmist: "I am wearied with calling, my throat is parched" (Ps 69:4).

How often have we been deaf to God's calls? Yet, even after our repeated sins, God stands at the door and knocks. God follows sinners like a rejected lover, begging them not to destroy themselves. St. Paul echoed the spirit of our merciful Father when he wrote: "We implore you, in Christ's name, be reconciled to God!" (2 Cor 5:20)

St. John Chrysostom says that it is not God, but the sinner who refuses to be reconciled.

God Receives

A leader who has been betrayed will not even deign to look at the rebel who comes to him seeking pardon. God does not act that way. He cannot turn away, for he himself invites us and promises to receive us. "Return, says the Lord, I will not remain angry with you; for I am merciful" (Jer 3:12).

Consider with what love and tenderness God embraces the returning sinner! He describes himself as the Good Shepherd — and tells us that there is joy in heaven over one sinner who does penance.

He portrays this love and tenderness even more graphically in the story of the prodigal son, in which he pictures himself as the father who races to greet and warmly embrace the son who had left his father's house.

He even promises that if sinners repent he will

forget their sins, just as if they had never offended him. "But if the wicked man turns away from all the sins he committed, if he keeps all my statutes and does what is right and just, he shall surely live; he shall not die" (Ez 18:21).

"Come now, let us set things right," says the Lord. "Though your sins be like scarlet, they may become white as snow" (Is 1:18).

No, God does not know how to despise a humble and contrite heart.

Prayer

Oh my God, it is only through your mercy that I am not now in hell, but at your feet seeking to know your will for me. I hear you say, "You shall love the Lord with all your heart." Help me to resist your calls no longer, to give you no more displeasure, and to accept with deepest gratitude your mercy and love. Amen.

Chapter 12

Remember the Reward

"I tell you truly: you will weep and mourn while the world rejoices; you will grieve for a time, but your grief will be turned to joy" (Jn 16:20).

Let us try to bear patiently all the afflictions of this life, offering them to God in union with the sufferings of Jesus Christ, and thus strengthening ourselves with the hope of heaven.

All our afflictions, our sorrows, our tears, will some-day come to an end, and will in fact become the source of our joy and happiness in heaven. "Your grief," says Jesus, "will be turned into joy!"

How can we understand or describe, while still on earth, the happiness of heaven? Even the most enlightened saints of God could not give us an idea of what God has prepared for his servants.

David could say only: "How lovely is your dwelling place, O Lord of hosts!" (Ps 84:2) St. Paul who was lifted up into heaven could say that its delights were as "words which cannot be uttered, words which no man may speak" (2 Cor 12:4). And he added that "eye has not seen, ear has not heard, nor has it so much as dawned on man what God has prepared for those who love him" (1 Cor 2:9). St. Teresa had a short glimpse of one hand of Jesus and was struck senseless by its beauty. St. Francis once heard a heavenly sound which sounded like a single note of an angelic violin, and almost died of joy!

It is impossible for us to understand the happiness of heaven, because we can think only in terms of earthly enjoyments. If a horse were capable of reasoning and were promised a rich feast from his owner, he would imagine it to consist of the choicest hay and oats. Our concept of heaven is formed in the same way.

What will heaven be like?

In heaven there is no sickness or infirmity, no poverty, no distress. There are no wars, persecutions, jealousies, envies. In that kingdom of love, all love one another tenderly. Each rejoices in the good of the other as if it were his own.

There is no fear, no anxiety; for those in heaven are confirmed in grace and can no longer sin or lose God. For what makes heaven, the essential good of heaven, is God himself. The reward which he promises us is not merely the beauty, the harmony, and all the other joys of this eternal city. The chief reward is God himself — that is, to see and love him face-to-face. " . . . I will make your reward very great" (Gn 15:1).

In our present state we cannot comprehend the delight of seeing God face-to-face. But we may form some notion of it by remembering that divine love is so captivating that even in this life it has sometimes caused certain of the saints to be bodily elevated from the earth.

St. Philip Neri was once so lifted up while still gripping the bench he had grasped to prevent it. St. Peter Alcantara was also elevated, and the tree which he held on to was torn from its roots.*

What peace, what sweetness often comes upon a person when in prayer he receives the goodness, the

*Editor's Note: St. Alphonsus himself had this unusual experience of being elevated while preaching on the love of God for us.

mercy of God, or the love which Jesus has shown men! Such a person almost faints for joy. Yet in this life we do not, see God as he is. "Now we see indistinctly, as in a mirror; then we shall see face-to-face . . . " (1 Cor 13:12).

In this life there is a veil before our eyes, and we see God only through the eyes of faith. What will be our joy when the veil is removed and we then see God face-to-face. His infinite beauty, his greatness, his perfection, his infinite love for us — all this we will enjoy forever!

On earth, one of the greatest afflictions for those who truly love God is the fear of not loving him enough, or of losing him. But in heaven, we will be certain that we love God and he loves us.

Furthermore, our love will be constantly augmented by the increased knowledge we will have of the magnitude of God's love — in becoming man and dying for us, in giving us himself as food in the Eucharist. Then, too, we will see how many graces God gave us in life; how he delivered us from so many temptations; how much patience he showed by enduring our many weaknesses and sins; how merciful he was to us in giving us so many lights, so many chances, so much love.

In heaven we will forever enjoy a happiness which as eternity moves on will always be as new as the first moment of eternity. We shall be always satisfied yet always thirsty. Forever hungry, yet always satiated with delights. Because the desire of heaven begets no pain, and its possession produces no tedium or ennui. In seeing God face-to-face, we will be so inebriated with love that we will lose ourselves in God. We will forget all about ourselves, and think only of loving, praising, blessing this infinite Good we possess forever!

When the crosses and pains of this life afflict us, let us animate ourselves with the hope of heaven. Let us remember that if we remain faithful to God, all these sorrows, miseries, and fears will one day end, and we shall enter heaven where we shall enjoy complete happiness forever.

The saints already await us, Mary expects us, and Jesus is there with a crown in his hands to make us kings in that eternal kingdom!

Prayer

My Jesus, you have taught me this prayer: Thy kingdom come! Lord, I do now pray that your kingdom may come into my heart, so that you may possess it entirely, and that I may possess you forever!

You have spared nothing to save me and win my love; take me then, and let my salvation consist in loving you always in this life and in the next. Keep your hand upon me that I may never more offend you.

O Mary, my Mother, assist me. Do not permit me to be lost, but obtain for me perseverance in my love for your Son, that heaven may be mine for all eternity!

Chapter 13
Accepting God's Will

"Over all these virtues put on love, which binds the rest together and makes them perfect" (Col 3:14).

The Superior Virtue

All spiritual life and all perfection consists in loving God. However, perfect love means accepting God's will. St. Denis says that the principle effect of love is to unite the will of the lovers, so that they have one heart and one will. It is for this reason that whatever we do — our actions, our prayers and Communions, even our gifts to the poor — will please God only if they are in conformity with his will. If they are not in accord with his will, they are not good works; they are defective and deserve no reward.

Jesus came from heaven principally to give us the example of conforming to God's will. St. Paul describes it in this way: "Wherefore, on coming into the world, Jesus said: 'Sacrifice and offering you did not desire, but a body you have prepared for me ' " (Heb 10:5). Jesus himself frequently declared that he came on earth to do his Father's will. " . . . It is not to do my own will that I have come down from heaven, but to do the will of him who sent me" (Jn 6:38). He went forth to die out of loving obedience to the Father's will. "But the world must know that I love the Father and do as the Father has commanded me . . . " (Jn 14:31).

Jesus also accepts as his own those who do the Father's will. "There are my mother and my brothers. Whoever does the will of my heavenly Father is brother and sister and mother to me" (Mt 12:50). And he teaches us to pray to do God's will on earth as the saints do it in heaven. "Thy will be done on earth as it is in heaven."

An act of perfect resignation to God's will is enough to make you a saint. When Paul was persecuting the early Christians, Jesus appeared to him, enlightened him, and converted him. All Saul offered was to do the divine will. Jesus said: "Get up and go into the city, where you will be told what to do" (Acts 9:6). Jesus constantly called him a "vessel of election" and an "apostle." "The Lord said . . . : 'You must go! This man is the instrument I have chosen to bring my name to the Gentiles and their kings and to the people of Israel' " (Acts 9:15). The person who fasts, gives alms, or mortifies himself for God's sake gives only a part of himself to God. But the one who gives his will to God gives himself entirely to God. All that God asks of us is our heart, that is, our will. "My son, give me your heart, and let your eyes keep to my ways" (Prov 23:26).

In one word, to do God's will must be the purpose of all our desires, our devotions, our meditations, our Holy Communions, etc. And the purpose of all our prayers must be to obtain from God the grace to do his will. We must always pray for the light and strength to be conformed to God's will in everything, but especially in accepting what goes against self-love. St. John Avila says that a single "Blessed be God" in adversity is better than six thousand acts of thanksgiving in prosperity.

When and Where to Accept God's Will

We must accept God's will not only in the crosses and adversities which come directly from God — for example, sickness, loss of loved ones through death, desolation of spirit — but also in those which come indirectly from God, that is, through people. We must remember that when people deliberately harm or hurt us, God does not will their sin, but he does will our humiliation and loss. Whatever happens takes place by the divine will. "Good and evil, life and death, poverty and riches are from the Lord" (Eccl 11:14). In a word, all things — blessings as well as misfortunes — come from God.

Crosses that come to us are called "evils" because we call them such and make them so. If we accepted them as we ought — resigned to the fact that they come from God — they would become for us not evils but blessings. This is what the saints of God do. What did Job say when they told him the Sabeans had stolen his property? "Naked I came forth from my mother's womb, and naked shall I go back again. The Lord gave and the Lord has taken away; blessed be the name of the Lord!" He did not say, the Lord gave and the Sabeans took away! And he even blessed the Lord knowing that it had happened by his will (See Jb 1:13-21).

We must do the same when crosses or sufferings come to us. Let us accept them as coming from God, patiently, even joyfully, as the apostles did. "The apostles for their part left the Sanhedrin full of joy that they had been judged worthy of ill-treatment for the sake of the Name" (Acts 5:41).

If we wish to enjoy continual interior peace, let us try from now on to accept the Father's will saying with Jesus, "Father, it is true. You have graciously willed it so" (Mt 11:26). In all our meditations, Communions, prayers, Visits, let us ask the Lord to help us conform to his will and continually offer ourselves to him. St. Teresa offered herself to God frequently each day that he might dispose of her as he wished.

Accepting God's will makes you truly happy. Conformity to God's will brings lasting peace. "No harm befalls the just, but the wicked are overwhelmed with misfortune" (Prov 12:21). Our greatest happiness comes when all our desires are fulfilled. But if we desire only what God wills, then we have all we want, because whatever happens, happens through God's will.

When we remain conformed to God's will and resigned to whatever he wants or does — like a man standing above the clouds, watching the tempest raging below — that peace which St. Paul describes as "surpassing all understanding and which exceeds all worldly pleasures" descends upon us. "Then God's own peace, which is beyond all understanding, will stand guard over your hearts and minds, in Christ Jesus" (Phil 4:7).

Crosses and sufferings may indeed produce some pain to body and mind, but still peace will reign. "In the same way, you are sad for a time, but I shall see you again; then your hearts will rejoice with a joy no one can take from you" (Jn 16:22). Those who oppose God's will must still bear the cross, but without fruit and without peace. "God is wise in heart and mighty in strength; who has withstood him and remained unscratched?" (Jb 9:4)

God wills only our good, our happiness. He wishes to see us become saints, that we may be content in this life and happy in the next. "It is God's will that you grow in holiness: that you abstain from immorality" (1 Thes 4:3). His crosses work for our good. Even punishments from God are inflicted on us not for our destruction but that we might amend and eventually win heaven. "Not for vengeance did the Lord put them in the crucible to try their hearts, nor has he done so with us. It is by way of admonition that he chastises those who are close to him" (Jdt 8:27).

St. Peter tells us: "Cast all your cares on him because he cares for you" (1 Pt 5:7). Jesus confirmed this saying to St. Catherine of Sienna, "Think of me and I will always think of you."

We ought to pray, therefore, not that God's will become our will, but that we may do his. If we do so, then we will lead a truly happy life and die a happy death. For he who dies entirely resigned to the divine will is morally assured of salvation.

Here are some short sayings from Scripture which will help to keep us united with God's will:

"What is it I must do?" (Acts 22:10)

" . . . I am the servant of the Lord. Let it be done to me as you say . . . " (Lk 1:38).

"I am yours; save me, for I have sought your precepts" (Ps 119:94).

"Father it is true. You have graciously willed it so" (Mt 11:26).

And above all, let the words of the *Our Father* be so dear to us that we will repeat them often in life and at the hour of death — "your will be done on earth as it is in heaven."

Prayer

My Jesus, you have sacrificed yourself and have died for me. But how have I repaid your love? I thank you for having had so much patience with me and for giving me time to repair my ingratitude. I am sorry, my Savior, and from now on I wish to do whatever is pleasing to you. I accept now the death you wish to send me, with all the pains and sufferings that may accompany it. Grant that during life I may be resigned to the arrangements of your divine Providence and that, when death comes, I may accept your holy will. I wish to die saying, "Your will be done."

Appendix

Some Prayers
of St. Alphonsus

Declaration for a Happy Death

My God, prostrate in your presence, I adore you; and I intend to make the following statement, as if I were on the point of passing from this life to eternity:

My Lord, because you are infallible truth and have revealed it to the holy Church, I believe in the mystery of the Most Holy Trinity — Father, Son, and Holy Spirit: three Persons, but only one God, who eternally rewards the just with heaven and punishes sinners with hell. I believe that the second Person — that is, the Son of God — became man and died for the salvation of men; and I believe all that the holy Church believes. I thank you for having made me a Christian; and I profess that in this holy faith I wish to live and die.

My God, my Hope, trusting in your promises, I hope from your mercy, not through my merits but through the merits of Jesus Christ, for the pardon of my sins, perseverance in your grace, and after this life, for the glory of heaven. And should the devil, at death, tempt me to despair at the sight of my sins, I profess that I wish always to hope in you, my Lord, and that I wish to die in the loving arms of your goodness.

O God, worthy of infinite love, I love you with my whole heart, and more than I love myself; I profess that I wish to die making an act of love, that thus I may continue to love you for eternity in heaven; this I seek and desire from you. And if, O Lord, instead of loving you, I have till now despised your infinite goodness, I am sorry for it with my whole heart, and I profess that I wish to die regretting and detesting forever the offences I have inflicted on you. I want rather to die than to commit another sin. And, for the love of you, I pardon all who have offended me.

O my God, I accept death and all the pains that will accompany my death. I unite them to the sorrows and to the death of Jesus Christ, and submit them to your supreme dominion in satisfaction for my sins. O Lord, for the sake of your divine Son's own great sacrifice offered on the altar of the Cross, accept this sacrifice of my life which I offer to you. I now, in anticipation of my death, resign myself entirely to your divine will, confessing that I wish to die with these words on my lips: O Lord, your will be done.

Most holy Virgin Mary, my advocate and my Mother, you, after God, are and shall be my hope and consolation at the hour of death. I now invoke you and pray you to assist me at that great moment. My dear Queen, do not ever abandon me. Come, then, take my soul and present it to your Son. From this moment I await you, and hope to die under your protection and prostrate at your feet. My protector, St. Joseph, St. Michael the archangel, my angel-guardian, my holy advocates, please be there to assist me in that last battle with hell.

And you, my crucified Love — my Jesus who, to obtain for me a good death, voluntarily chose so painful a death — remember at that hour that I am one of the sheep which you have purchased with your blood. O my Savior — who alone can console me and save me at that hour when everyone on this earth will have abandoned me, and when no friend will be able to assist me — make me worthy at that time to receive you in the Eucharist. Do not permit me to lose you forever, to remain eternally at a distance from you. No, my beloved Savior, since I now embrace you, receive me then into your holy wounds. At my last breath I intend to breathe forth my soul into the loving wound in your side, saying now, in anticipation of that moment: Jesus and Mary, I give you my heart and soul.

Happy suffering, to suffer for God! Happy death, to die in the Lord!

Prayer for a Happy Death

My Lord Jesus Christ, by that bitterness which you endured on the Cross when your blessed soul was separated from your most sacred body, have pity on my sinful soul when it leaves my body to enter into eternity.

O Mary! By that grief which you experienced on Calvary in seeing Jesus expire on the Cross before your eyes, obtain for me a good death, that loving Jesus and you, my Mother, in this life, I may attain heaven where I shall love you for all eternity.

Prayer to Obtain Final Perseverance

Eternal Father, I humbly adore and thank you for having created me and for having redeemed me. I thank you for having made me a Christian by giving me the true faith and for adopting me as your child in Baptism. I thank you for having given me time to repent after my many sins, and for having pardoned all my offenses. I renew my sorrow for them, because I have displeased you. I thank you also for having preserved me from falling again, as I would have done if you had not held me up and saved me. But my enemies do not cease fighting against me, nor will they until I die. If you do not help me continually, I will lose your grace again. I, therefore, pray for perseverance till death. Your Son Jesus has promised that you will give us whatever we ask for in his name. By the merits of Jesus Christ, I beg you, for myself and for all those who are in your grace, the grace of never more being separated from your love. May we always love you in this life and in the next. Mary, Mother of God, pray to Jesus for me.

Prayer for the Graces Necessary for Salvation

Eternal Father, your Son has promised that you will grant us all the graces which we ask for in his name. In the name and merits of Jesus Christ, I ask the following graces for myself and for all mankind.

Please give me a lively faith in all that the Church teaches. Enlighten me that I may know the vanity of the goods of this world and the immensity of the infinite good that you are. Make me also see the deformity of the sins I have committed, that I may humble myself and detest them as I should.

Give me a firm confidence of receiving pardon for my sins, holy perseverance, and the glory of heaven, through the merits of Jesus Christ and the intercession of Mary.

Give me a great love for you that will detach me from the love of this world and of myself, so that I may love none other but you.

I beg of you a perfect resignation to your will. I offer myself entirely to you, that you might do with me and all that belongs to me as you please.

I beg of you a great sorrow for my sins.

I ask you to give me the spirit of true humility and meekness, that I may accept with peace and even with joy all the contempt, ingratitude, and ill-treatment I may receive. At the same time, I also ask you to give me perfect charity, which shall make me wish well to those who have done evil to me.

Give me love for the virtue of mortification, by which I may chastise my rebellious senses and oppose my self-love. Give me a great confidence in the Passion of Jesus Christ and in the intercession of Mary immaculate. Give me a great love for the Blessed Sacrament, and a tender devotion and love to your holy Mother. Give me, above all, holy perseverance and the grace always to pray for it, especially in time of temptation and at the hour of death.

Finally, I recommend to you the holy souls of purgatory, and in a special manner I recommend to you all those who hate me or who have in any way offended me; I beg you to render them good for the evil they have done or may wish to do me. Grant that, by your goodness, I may come one day to sing your mercies in heaven; for my hope is in the merits of your blood and in the patronage of Mary. Mary, Mother of God, pray to Jesus for me.

OTHER HELPFUL PUBLICATIONS FROM LIGUORI

Life Beyond Death
Reflections on Dying and Afterlife
by John C. Tormey

A warm, sympathetic book that takes a basic, understandable approach to a subject that is difficult for many to discuss, much less understand. Each page presents a separate thought or commentary on death, grief, mourning, dying — based on the author's personal experience and observations. This book combines sound psychology with a Christian viewpoint and presents death as a transformation, a continuance, rather than a cessation. **$1.50.**

Coping with Widowhood
by Frances Caldwell Durland

In this book, a widow tells her own story of how she learned to "cope" with the pain, the shock, the bewilderment of losing a mate, a life's partner. To her, coping meant growing through suffering to find again the richness, fullness, and beauty of *life* — even if it meant a life alone. **$1.50.**

Dealing with Depression
A Whole-Person Approach
by Russell Abata, C.SS.R., and William Weir, Ed.D.
The authors have researched this subject thoroughly and have provided practical helps and guidelines for those who are heavily burdened by the despair of depression. This book offers a sympathetic, sensitive look at a difficult problem faced by many today. **$3.50.**

Inner Calm
by Dr. Paul DeBlassie III
In today's hurried, harried world, we all long for a greater sense of peace and joy, a true inner calm. This book addresses that need and explains the beauty and hope of the "Jesus Prayer." In this "Christian answer to modern stress," the author shares with the reader a wealth of healing experiences and offers an invitation to discover the true meaning of inner calm in today's world. **$3.95.**

See ordering information on page 64.

PAMPHLETS
50¢ each

Comfort for Those in Mourning
How to Cope with Unanswered Prayers
How to Have Confidence in God
How to Tell Your Child About Death
Is There Life After Death?
When You're Angry at God
Why Does God Let Me Suffer?

Order from your local bookstore
or write to:
Liguori Publications
Box 060, Liguori, Missouri 63057

(Please add 75¢ for postage and
handling for first item ordered and
25¢ for each additional item.)*
**For single pamphlet order, send 50¢
plus stamped, self-addressed envelope.*